Also by David Taylor II:

My Alphabet is Colorful!

My Alphabet is Musical!

My Alphabet is Yummy!

Diary of a Chocolate Midas

Diary of a Smart Black Kid: Sixth Grade

Dear God: Why Doesn't Broccoli taste like Chocolate?

www.DavidTaylor2.net

Follow me on Twitter: @dt2author

My Alphabet is My Pet!

Book 4 of the Series: My Alphabet Is...

Text and Illustrations
@Copyright David Taylor II
1st Ed 2019
All Rights Reserved.

1st Edition, Softcover
Published in 2019 by
HODT Books, PO Box 693
Skokie, IL 60076-0693
ISBN 978-1-7336248-4-8
www.HODTBooks.com

All rights reserved. No part of this book may be reproduced or transmitted in any form, or by any means, electronic, mechanical, digital, photocopying, recording, or by any storage and retrieval information system, or any technology created in the future relative to the publishing date of this book, without the express written permission of the publisher.

This book is a work of fiction. Names, characters, places and incidents either are products of the author's imagination or used fictitiously. Any resemblance to actual persons, living or dead, events or locales, is purely and entirely coincidental

Printed in the USA
10 9 8 7 6 5 4 3 2 1

Dedicated to
Beginning Readers
that love
their pets!

My Alphabet is My Pet!

David Taylor II

HODT BOOKS, INC.

SKOKIE, IL

A is for Aardvark

C is for Cat

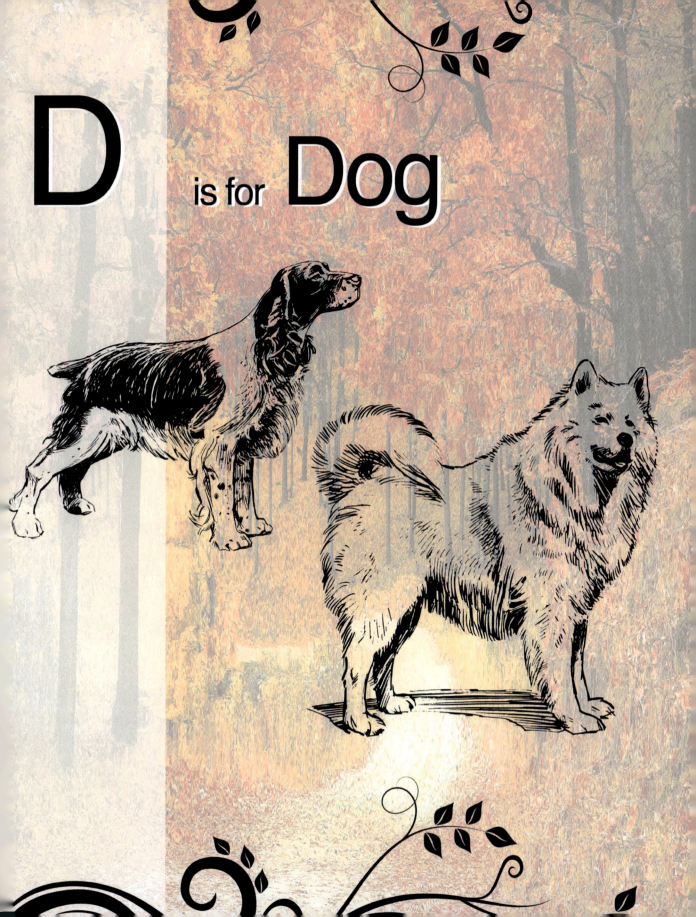

E is for Eagle

G is for Goat

H is for Hamster

L is for Ladybug

P is for Panda

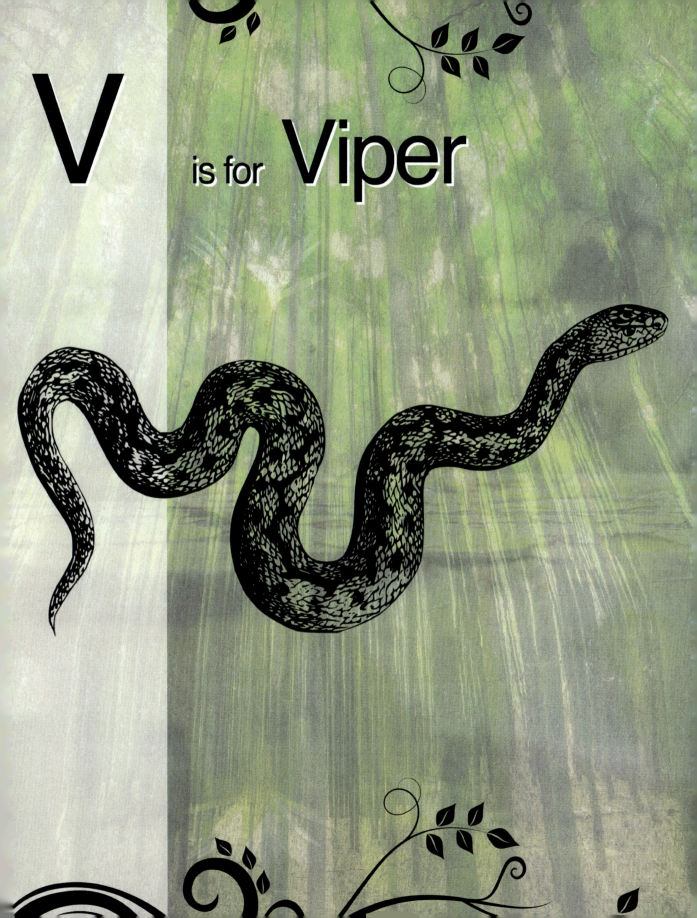

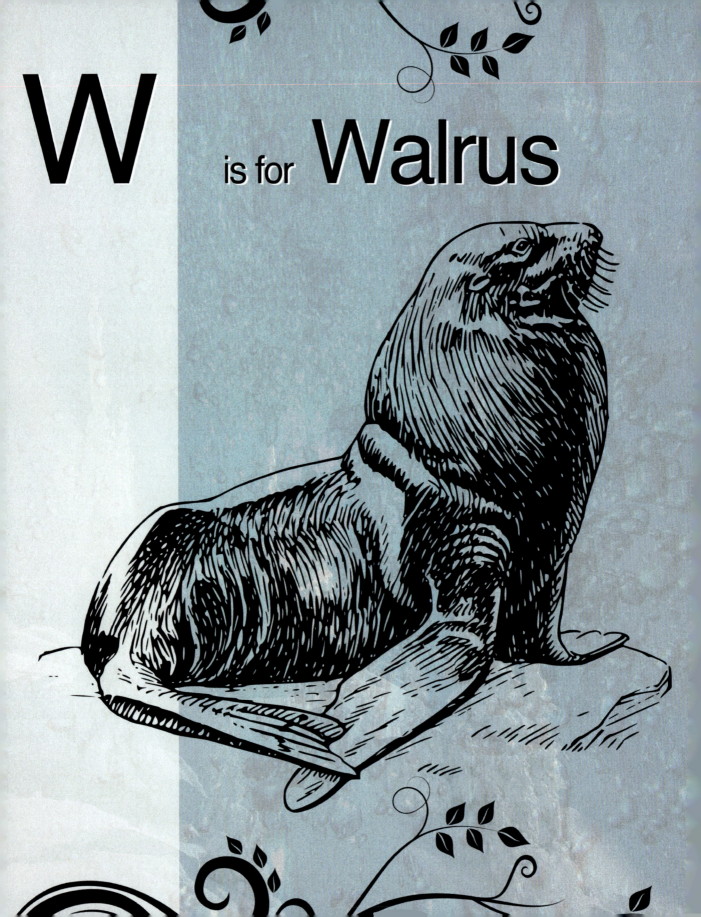

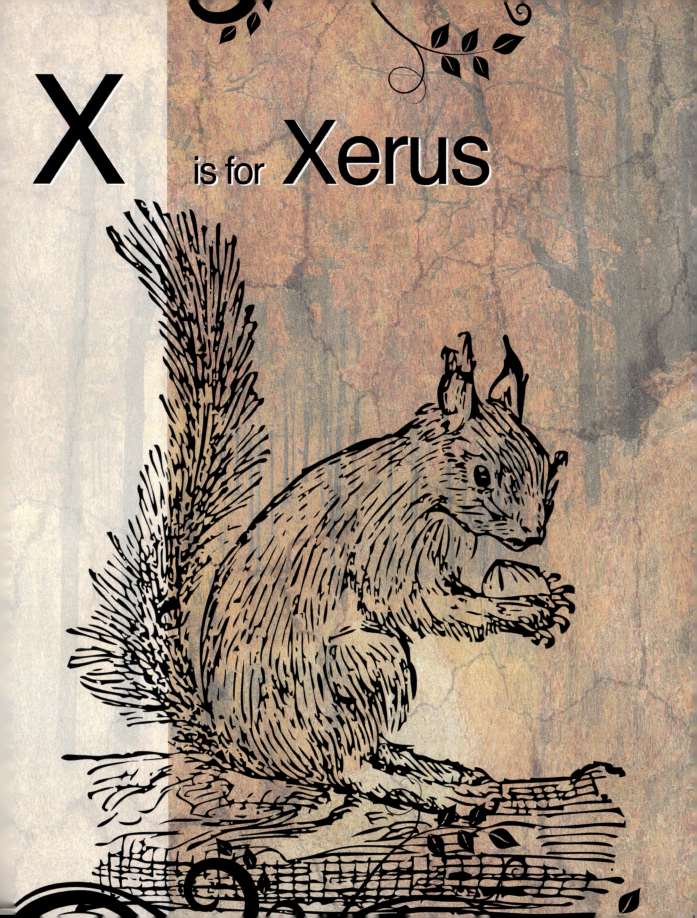

Y is for Yak

David Taylor II
loves to write books,
make music,
eat pizza,
and create superhero comics.
He was born in Evanston, IL

www.DavidTaylor2.net

Follow on Twitter: @dt2author

Made in the USA
Middletown, DE
09 May 2019